KENYA

Wambui Kairi

RSVP
RAINTREE
STECK-VAUGHN
P U B L I S H E R S
A Steck-Vaughn Company

Austin, Texas
www.steck-vaughn.com

Other titles:

Brazil ● The Caribbean ● China ● France ● India
Israel ● Japan ● Italy ● Mexico ● West Africa

Cover photograph: A fruit seller with a basket of ripe bananas

Title page: A Samburu mother with her newborn baby

Contents page: A woman preparing *ugali*, a dish made from cornmeal

Published by Raintree Steck-Vaughn Publishers, an imprint of Steck-Vaughn Company

Printed in Italy. Bound in the United States.
1 2 3 4 5 6 7 8 9 0 04 03 02 01 00

Library of Congress Cataloging-in-Publication Data
Kairi, Wambui.
Kenya / Wambui Kairi.
    p.   cm.—(Food and festivals)
    Includes bibliographical references and index.
    ISBN 0-7398-1373-0
    1. Cookery, Kenyan—Juvenile literature.
    2. Food habits—Kenyal—Juvenile literature.
    3. Festivals—Kenya—Juvenile literature.
    I. Title.
    TX725.K39K35   1999
    394.1'096762—dc21   99-27164

CONTENTS

Kenya and Its Food

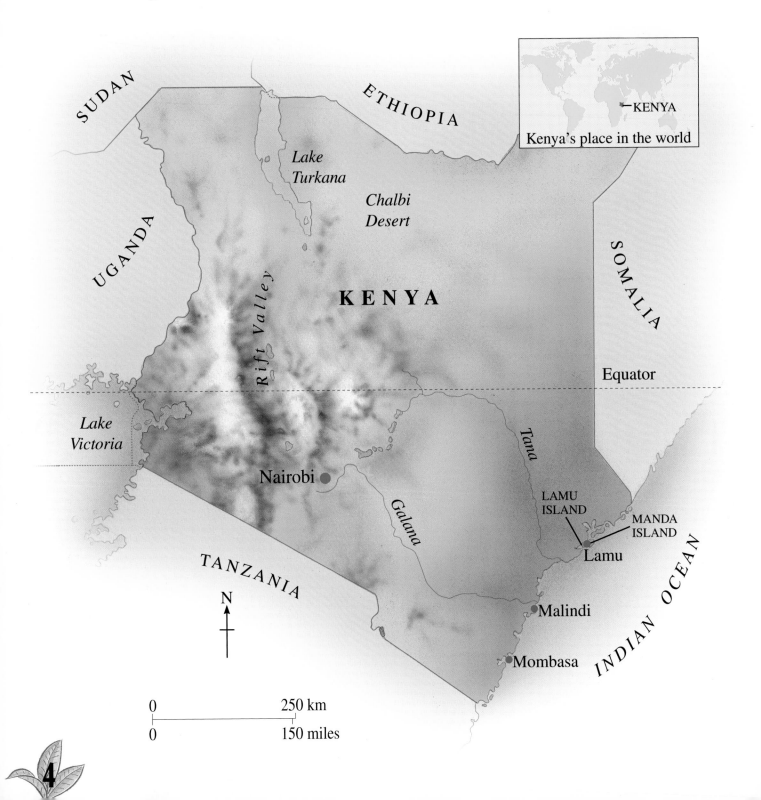

SUDAN

ETHIOPIA

UGANDA

Lake Turkana

Chalbi Desert

KENYA

SOMALIA

Rift Valley

Equator

Lake Victoria

Tana

Galana

LAMU ISLAND

MANDA ISLAND

Lamu

Nairobi

TANZANIA

N

Malindi

Mombasa

INDIAN OCEAN

KENYA

Kenya's place in the world

| 0 | 250 km |
| 0 | 150 miles |

CATTLE, GOATS, AND SHEEP

These animals provide meat and milk. In the cities, there is always a scramble to buy live goats to slaughter for the Christmas and New Year's feasts.

NUTS

Peanuts and cashew nuts are important ingredients in Kenyan food. Peanuts grow underground. They can be roasted or made into a paste for sauces or peanut butter.

VEGETABLES

Leafy, green kale is a cheap and very popular vegetable. Kale, carrots, and other vegetables are a colorful sight piled high on market stands.

TEA

Everyone in Kenya drinks tea, and much tea is sold to other countries, too. Thousands of tea pickers are needed to harvest the leaves.

GRAINS AND SEEDS

Cornmeal can be used to make *ugali*, and millet is used for porridge (a hot cereal). *Simsim* (sesame seeds) are sometimes used to make cookies.

FRUITS

Bananas, mangoes, and pineapples are just some of the many fruits that grow well in Kenya. During the mango season, there are often yellow juice stains on children's clothes.

Food and Farming

Kenya is a tropical country in eastern Africa. It has a coastline on the Indian Ocean, and the equator runs almost through the middle of the country. The climate in Kenya varies from place to place.

Northern and northeastern Kenya are very hot and dry, and so are parts of the Rift Valley. The peoples who live here include the Maasai, Somali, and Samburu. They keep camels, goats, and cattle. They move from place to place, looking for fresh pasture and water for their animals.

▼ Kenyan herders with their camels

Along the coast, the climate is hot and wet. It is hot around Lake Victoria, too, but less humid. Tropical fruits, such as mangoes, pawpaws, and pineapples, grow well in these areas.

If you took a train from the city of Mombasa, on the coast, to the capital, Nairobi, you would notice the difference in the temperature. Nairobi is on the edge of the cool, wet highlands. Most of Kenya's crops are produced in this area. The climate is especially good for growing tea and coffee.

▲ Traders selling peanuts and cashew nuts. Cashew nuts are picked from trees that grow only along the coast.

▼ A tea picker at work. Only two leaves and a bud are taken from each stem of the bushes, so the tea cannot be harvested by machine.

7

Staple foods

Vegetables and grains are the traditional staple foods in Kenya. Kale, which is called *sukumawiki* (say sue-coo-ma-wickie), is eaten with many meals. It is cheap and full of vitamins. Potatoes are becoming a staple food, too, especially in the towns and cities. French fries served with chicken and fish provide a cheap lunch for city workers and students.

SUKUMAWIKI, MY LOVE

Kale, or *sukumawiki,* is so popular that there is a poem in its honor:

"All this I am saying
To all you listeners
Is in praise of *sukumawiki*, my love.
Whenever I am hungry, ready is *sukumawiki.*
Sukumawiki, my love, may the Lord bless you."

(Translated from the Kiswahili poem "*Sukumawiki Kipenzi*" written by Ezekiel Tsinalo)

▼ Two women clear the weeds from the young kale plants in their vegetable garden.

◄ Farmers harvesting rice by hand, near Mombasa

▼ A woman prepares a large pot of batter to make *ugali* (corn cake).

Rice is grown in central and western Kenya and near the coast. Rice needs warm weather and much water to grow, so the fields have to be flooded when the rice is planted. Millet, cow peas, and black beans are grown in central and western Kenya. They can be stored for a long time and eaten during the dry season.

Corn is grown in most parts of the country. The grains can be dried and ground up to produce cornmeal. The cornmeal is used to make porridge and *ugali* (corn cake). *Ugali* is eaten with vegetable-and-meat stew, or with fish.

◄ A herder with his goats. Each goat is marked with a symbol to show which family owns it.

Cattle and poultry

Beef and goat are the meats most often eaten in Kenya. For the herders, meat is the most important part of their everyday diet. Besides eating the meat, the herders sometimes drain a little blood from the necks of live goats and cattle and drink it. It is a good way to get nourishment from their animals without having to kill them.

Chicken is a delicacy in western Kenya. It is the custom for each member of the family to eat a different part of the bird. The men eat the thighs, the women eat the breast meat, boys get the head and neck, and girls are given the wings.

▼ A herder carefully shoots an arrow into a bullock's neck to drain some of its blood.

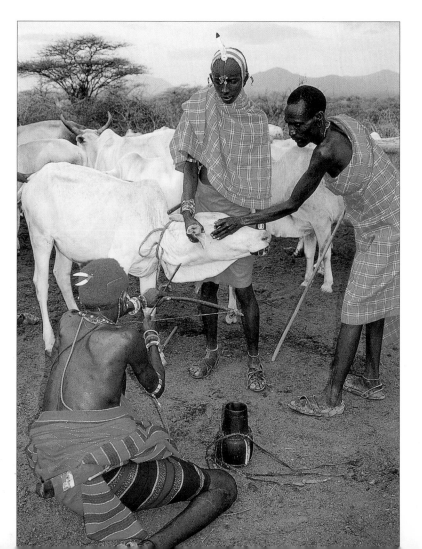

Fish

Fish is an important food for people living along the coast and around the lakes. Most Kenyans love tilapia, a very tasty fish. Tilapia is silver-black and grows to about 14 in. (35 cm) long. There are many ways of preparing fish. Fried fish is especially popular.

▼ A girl cooks fish, caught in nearby Lake Turkana. She is using palm leaves as fuel, instead of wood.

NYAMA, NYAMA, NYAMA

Nyama, nyama, nyama is a game that means "meat, meat, meat." Ten people sit in a circle and choose a leader, who calls out the names of different animals.

If the animal that is called out can be eaten, everyone jumps up. If you jump up when an animal that cannot be eaten is called out, you are out!

People and Religions

The people of Kenya are mostly Africans, but there are also Asians, Arabs, and Europeans. Arab traders were the first non-Africans to arrive in Kenya. Some settled around Mombasa and on Lamu and Manda islands. They brought the Muslim religion to Kenya.

Later, in the fifteenth century, Portuguese explorers arrived. They were Christians. At the end of the nineteenth century, the British took control of Kenya and helped spread Christianity to more people. They also brought followers of the Hindu religion from India to work for them. In Kenya today, 83 percent of the people are Christians, and there are also many Hindus and Muslims.

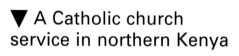

▼ A Catholic church service in northern Kenya

KENYA'S CLANS

African peoples moved into Kenya from other parts of the continent—a period known as the "great migrations." The different groups settled in the areas where they live today and formed smaller groups, called clans. For example, the Agikuyu people have nine clans, and one of these is called the Ambui clan.

Some peoples, such as the Maasai, Turkana, Ngiriama, and Ameru, follow traditional African religions. They believe in one, all-powerful God, although each of the peoples calls him by a different name, such as Mungu, Allah, or Ngai. They believe that the spirits of their ancestors can pass on to God their thanks and requests for help.

▲ This Kikuyu dancer is wearing an elaborate headdress and face paint because he is taking part in a religious ceremony.

13

Christmas

For Christian children in Kenya, December 25 is the most joyous day of the year. It is Christmas Day, when the birth of Jesus is celebrated. It is also the day when they get new clothes and shoes and have delicious food to eat. There may be extra gifts for children who have behaved well or done well at school.

CHRISTMAS CARDS

Kenyan Christmas cards used to be imported from Europe. They showed scenes such as Santa Claus in the snow, but most Kenyans had never seen snow. Now there are cards that show Santa Claus riding a camel in the desert. Others show baby Jesus wrapped in a traditional Kenyan cloth called a *kanga*.

◀ This boy's family has decorated the roof of their house with flowers for Christmas.

Christmas brings families together for a big party. The cities are almost deserted because many people prefer to celebrate at their family homes in the country.

Celebrations begin on December 24, which is Christmas Eve. Young people go from house to house, singing Christmas carols. Among the Agikuyu people of central Kenya, this tradition is called *murekio*, which means "messenger." The singers are bringing news of the birth of Jesus. They collect gifts, too, which they take to church on Christmas Day.

▲ Even this bus in Nairobi has been decorated for Christmas.

Christians practice ▶ Christmas carols.

◀ These children are dressed up for their Nativity play.

At church services on Christmas Eve, people act out the story of Jesus' birth. At their nativity plays they wear traditional African clothes and offer presents such as goats and baskets of grain. They sing African carols and songs to welcome a new baby. There is dancing and music.

▼ These three girls have brought goats to offer to the baby Jesus in a nativity play.

On Christmas day, most Christians go to church. It is mainly women who go to church throughout the year, but on this special day the men go too.

Wealthy visitors from the cities bring offerings of money to country churches. Poorer people bring fruit and grain. Their offerings are auctioned to raise money for the work of the church.

▲ These Maasai children have just been to a Christmas Day service in the church behind, where they played their drum.

▲ *Simsim* is the Kenyan word for sesame seeds. *Simsim* cookies are a Christmas treat in western Kenya. You can find out how to make them on the opposite page.

In the countryside, people go home after church to enjoy a feast. They visit their relatives and eat even more food. Everyone enjoys the treats that relatives from the cities bring home with them, such as cakes, fruit juices, and bread.

People who stay in the cities on Christmas go out for lunch in a restaurant or go on a picnic. Those who can afford to buy a goat to eat may have a barbecue. People living near the coast sometimes spend the day at the beach.

Simsim Cookies

INGREDIENTS

5 oz. (150 g) sesame seeds
6 Tablespoons brown sugar
2 Tablespoons boiling water
A pinch of salt

EQUIPMENT

1 greased cookie sheet
Oven mitts
Tablespoon
Mixing bowl

teakettle
Wax paper
Spatula
Spreader

Spread the sesame seeds on a greased cookie sheet and roast in a preheated oven at 375° F (190° C) for about 15 minutes until they are golden.

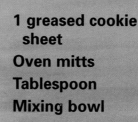

Heat some water in the teakettle. Put the sugar and salt in the bowl and add the 2 Tablespoons hot water. Mix together to make a smooth paste.

Stir the sesame seeds into the sugar paste. Spoon the mixture onto a cookie sheet lined with wax paper and spread it in a thin layer.

Let the cookie mixture harden in the refrigerator overnight. Then cut it into squares and eat the cookies as a snack.

Be careful when using ovens and hot water. Ask an adult to help you.

Ramadan and Id-ul-Fitr

During the month of Ramadan, Muslims fast during the hours of daylight. This means they eat and drink nothing from sunrise until sunset each day. Muslims fast as a way of remembering Allah's goodness to them, for providing them with food.

In the coastal towns of Malindi and Lamu, Muslims own most of the cafés, restaurants, and stores. During Ramadan, they usually close them for the whole month or open only in the evenings to serve *futari*, a light snack to break the fast.

The mosque in ▶
Nairobi, where
Muslims go to pray

Id-ul-Fitr

▲ Muslim women gather to pray at the end of Ramadan.

At the end of Ramadan, there is a day of celebration to break the fast, called Id-ul-Fitr. In Kenya, it is a public holiday. Muslim families exchange gifts, and husbands are expected to buy new *kangas* for their wives. Food is prepared for a feast. Spiced *pilaf* rice is usually served, and people also enjoy *simsim* cookies, dates, and candy called *halua*.

◀ Delicious snacks
are given to children
at the event.

In Mombasa, a party is held at the Makadara
Muslim Grounds to celebrate Id-ul-Fitr.
The fun goes on until late in the
evening. The streets are full
of people selling different
delicacies, from imported
dates to cassava chips
and bowls of ice cream
and other treats.

Children especially ▶
like *kaimati*, a small
doughnut coated
with sugar or grated
coconut. You can
find out how to
make *kaimati* on the
opposite page.

Kaimati

INGREDIENTS

1 cup lukewarm milk

1 teaspoon dried yeast

Pinch of sugar

1 beaten egg

3 ³/₄ cups unbleached flour

1 teaspoon salt

Oil for deep frying

Sugar or grated coconut

EQUIPMENT

Teaspoon

Measuring cup

Small bowl

Fork

Large bowl

Strainer

Wooden spoon

Clean dishtowel

Large pan for deep frying

Tablespoon

Kitchen tongs

Paper towel

Large plate

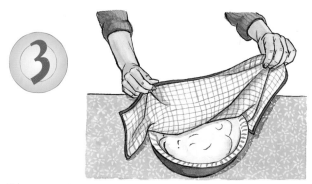

1 Pour the milk into a small bowl, then sprinkle the dried yeast and a pinch of sugar on the surface. Leave it for about 10 minutes until it looks frothy. Then beat it and stir in the egg.

2 Sift the flour and salt into the large bowl. Pour in the yeast mixture and stir it in. Form the mixture into a ball of dough and knead it on a floured surface for a few minutes.

3 Cover the bowl with a damp, clean, dishtowel and leave it for two hours. Check that the mixture has risen well, and ask an adult to deep-fry spoonfuls of the mixture until golden brown.

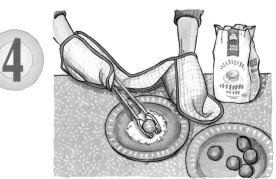

4 Lift the *kaimati* from the pan, and roll each one in sugar or grated coconut. Let them cool on paper towels.

Deep-frying can be very dangerous. You must ask an adult to help you.

Naming Ceremonies and Weddings

The birth of a child brings great joy. People come to see the new baby, bringing gifts such as food and baby clothes. Neighbors and relatives help with the cooking and cleaning so that the new mother can rest.

Among the Kikuyu people of the central province and the Rift Valley, a ceremony called *itega* is held to welcome a new baby. Only women take part in it. They sing songs in praise of the mother and baby. They take turns holding the baby and spitting on each other's foreheads, as a blessing.

◄ A mother with her new baby. She is a member of the Samburu people.

24

NAMES AND THEIR MEANINGS

Wayua
(Wa-Yoo-a)

A girl belonging to the Mukamba people, born during the dry, sunny season.

Mutuku
(Moo-TOO-coo)

A Mukamba boy, born during the night.

Njiraini
(N-jer-ARE-nee)

A boy belonging to the Mugikuyu people, born by the roadside.

Wambui
(Wom-BOO-ee)

A Mugikuyu girl belonging to the Ambui clan.

In some Kenyan communities, a ceremony is held to give the child a name. Names usually have a meaning that shows the time of day or the season when the child was born, or the place where he or she was born. Some names show who the child's ancestors were.

In country areas, ▶ people often bring firewood as a gift for a new mother.

Weddings

The Agikuyu people have a traditional wedding ceremony called *ngurario*. During the ceremony the bride is hidden by her girlfriends. Sometimes she disguises herself. The groom spends a lot of time looking for her, with the help of his friends. If he does not find her, then he does not marry her.

The bride and groom serve a special wine called *muratina* to the elders. A ram is slaughtered and specific parts are given to men and women. The young girls are given the ram's ears, to remind them to listen to their husbands! Instead of cutting a cake, the groom cuts the roasted leg of a ram.

A delicious tropical fruit punch ▶ is a treat for special celebrations. Find out how to make it on the opposite page.

▲ A bride, bridegroom, maid of honor, and best man (from right to left) bless the herd of goats they have been given as a wedding present.

Tropical Fruit Punch

INGREDIENTS (for 6)

2 bananas

4 oz. (100 g) washed strawberries

1 pawpaw, peeled

2 Tablespoons of brown sugar

1/3 cup orange juice

1/3 cup pineapple juice

1/3 cup mango juice

3 cups club soda

12 ice cubes

EQUIPMENT

Chopping board

Sharp knife

Large pitcher or bowl

Tablespoon

Measuring cup

Slice the bananas and cut the strawberries into halves. Put them in the pitcher or fruit bowl.

Chop the pawpaw into small cubes and put them in the jug or bowl. Add the brown sugar and stir it in gently.

Pour in the fruit juices.

Pour in the club soda and stir the mixture gently. Add the ice cubes and serve in tall glasses.

Be careful using knives. Ask an adult to help you.

Thanksgiving

Many Kenyans take part in thanksgiving celebrations. During Mass on New Year's Eve, Catholics give thanks for all the good things they have received in the past year. In September, Anglicans give thanks for the harvest. They take gifts of food to church.

Corn is often included because it is a staple food. The food is blessed and then given to the poor.

Followers of the traditional African religions give thanks to God whenever there is a good harvest and plenty of rain for their animals. During the thanksgiving ceremony, a ram or bull is sacrificed. Some meat is left under a tree as an offering to God.

◀ There is a recipe for this spicy corn dish on the opposite page.

Spicy Corn

INGREDIENTS (for 2)

2 ears of corn, washed

½ Teaspoon chili powder

½ teaspoon salt

1 large lemon

EQUIPMENT

Large saucepan
Kitchen tongs
Teaspoon
Small bowl

Sharp knife
Chopping board
Oven mitts
Plate

① Put the ears of corn into a saucepan of boiling water. Make sure the water covers them. Boil just until tender.

② Mix the chili powder with the salt in a small bowl. Cut the lemon into two round halves and remove the seeds.

③ Pour the chili/salt mixture onto the lemon halves. Squeeze the lemon so that the juice soaks the chili mixture.

④ Carefully take the corn out of the pan and put it on a large plate. Rub a lemon half over each ear of corn and eat them hot.

Be careful when using knives and hot pans. Ask an adult to help you.

Glossary

Allah The Muslim name for God.

Ancestors Family members who lived and died a long time ago.

Anglicans People belonging to a church similar to the established Church of England.

Auctioned Sold to the person who offers the highest price (instead of being sold for a fixed price, like goods in a supermarket).

Catholics Christians who are led by the Pope in Rome, Italy.

Climate The pattern of weather that an area usually has.

Equator The imaginary line that runs around the center of the earth, halfway between the North and South poles.

Humid The weather is humid when it is warm with much moisture in the air, although it is not actually raining.

Imported Brought in from another country.

Kanga A large cloth with traditional patterns printed on it. The Kanga can be worn like a dress.

Mass An important religious ceremony celebrated by Catholics.

Migration The movement of large numbers of people (or animals) from one place to another.

Muslims People who follow the religion called Islam.

Sacrificed Killed as an offering to God, as part of a religious ceremony.

Staple foods Foods that people eat with most everyday meals.

Tropical Between the Tropics of Cancer and Capricorn on the world map. Tropical areas have hot, wet weather all year round.

Ugali A savory dish made from cornmeal, usually eaten with stews.

Picture acknowledgments

Steve Benbow 5 (bottom right), 7; Chris Brown Educational 15 (bottom); Chapel Studios/Zul Mukhida 5 (bottom left), 18, 22 (bottom), 26 (bottom), 28; Robert Harding 5 (top left)/Thomasin Magor, 6/N.A. Callow, 10 (top)/Thomasin Magor; Images of Africa *cover*/Carla Signorini Jones, *title page*/Carla Signorini Jones, 5 (top right)/Carla Signorini Jones, 10 (bottom)/Carla Signorini Jones, 12/David Keith Jones, 16 (lower)/David Keith Jones, 24/Carla Signorini Jones, 25/David Keith Jones, 26 (top)/David Keith Jones; Impact 9 (top)/Caroline Penn; Peter Kenward *contents page*, 5 (center right), 7 (bottom), 9 (bottom), 22 (top); Oxfam (G. Sayer) 17; Panos 5 (center left)/ Betty Press, 8/Betty Press, 11/Lana Wong, 21/Betty Press; Ann & Bury Peerless 16 (top); Tony Stone Images 13/Art Wolfe; Tropix 14/J.Schmid, 15/J. Schmid; Zefa-Stockmarket 20/M.M. Lawrence. Fruit and vegetable artwork by Tina Barber. Map artwork on page 4 by Hardlines. Step-by-step recipe artwork by Judy Stevens.

Books to Read

Burch, Joanne J. *Kenya: Africa's Tamed Wilderness*. New York: Macmillan Children's Group, 1992.

Cremin, J. and Colm Regan. *Africa* (Continents). Austin, TX: Raintree Steck-Vaughn, 1997.

Dunne, Máiréad, Wambui Kairi, and Eric Nyanjom. *Kenya* (Country Insights). Austin, TX: Raintree Steck-Vaughn, 1998.

Gresko, Marcia. *Letters Home from Kenya*. Woodbridge, CT: Blackbirch, 1999.

King, David. *Kenya: Let's All Pull Together* (Exploring Cultures of the World). Tarrytown, NY: Benchmark Books, 1997.

Lerner Publications, Department of Geography. *Kenya in Pictures*. Minneapolis, MN: Lerner Publications, 1988.

Index

Page numbers in **bold** mean there is a photograph on the page.